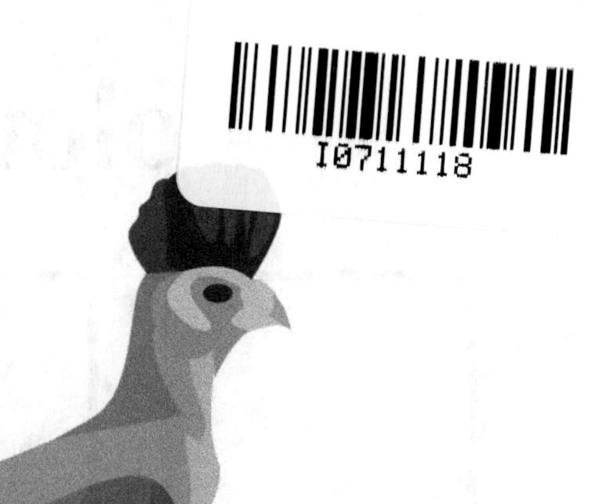

This Book Belongs To:

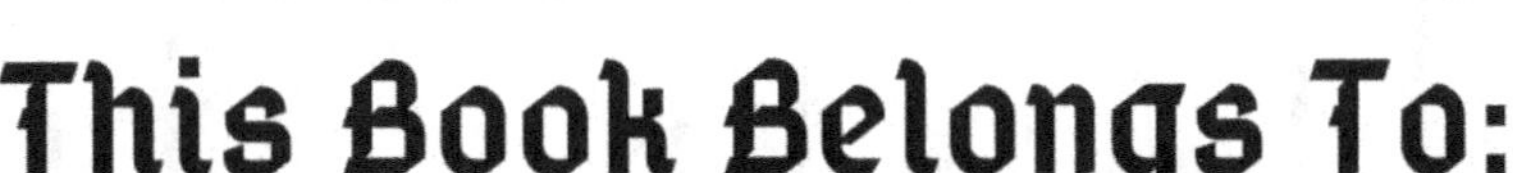

....

....

....

Coloring Test Page

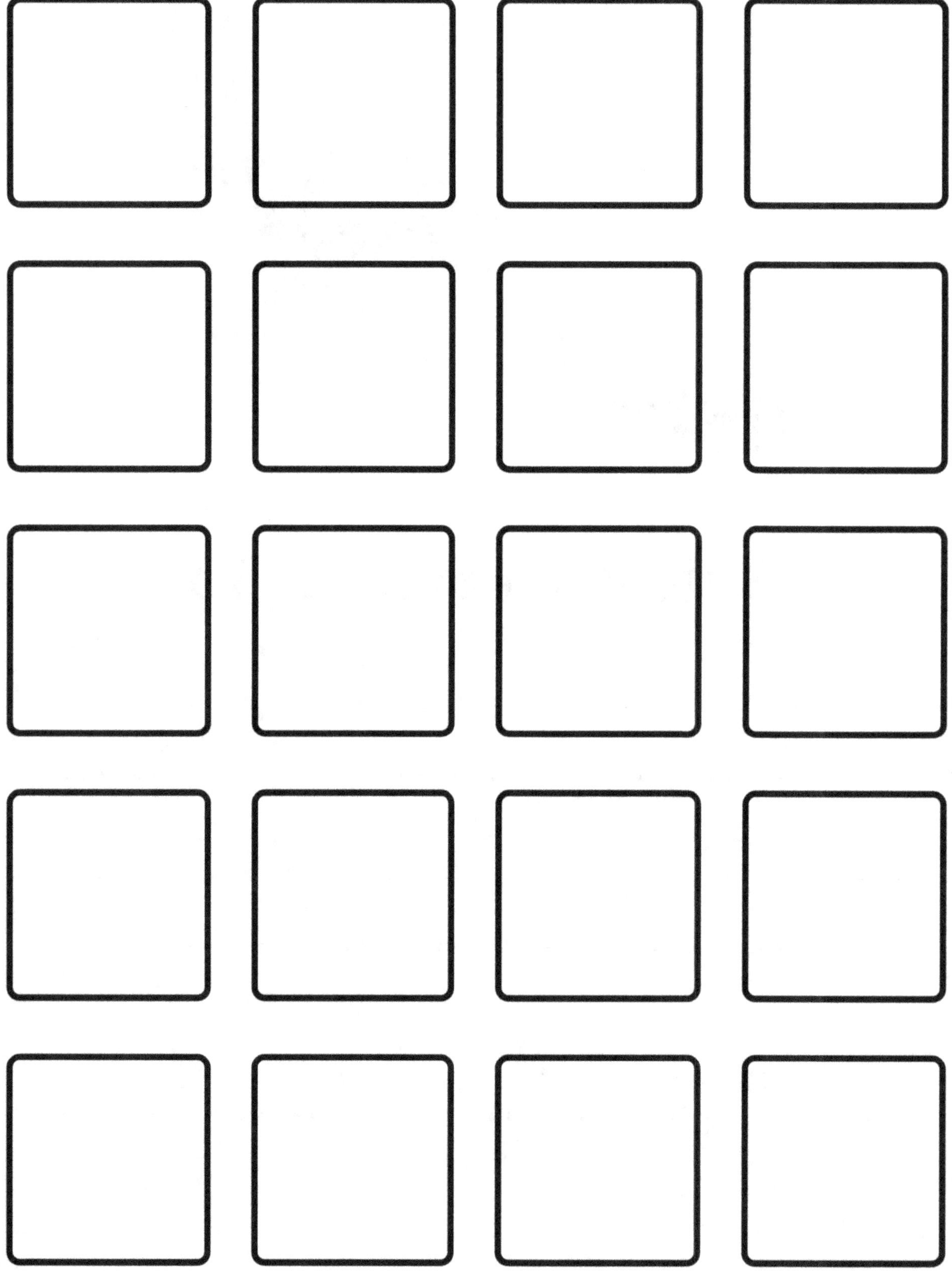

Coloring Test Page

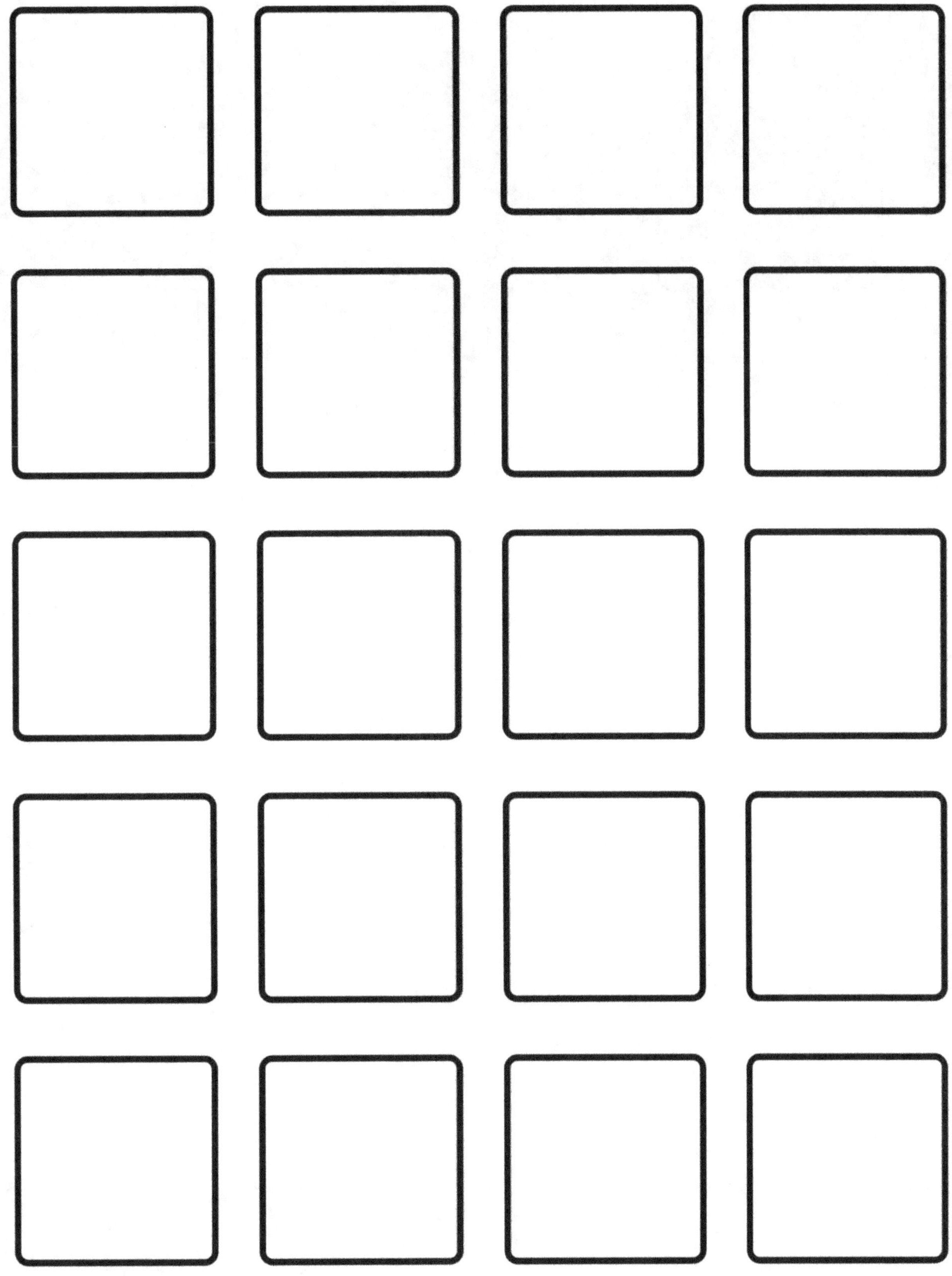

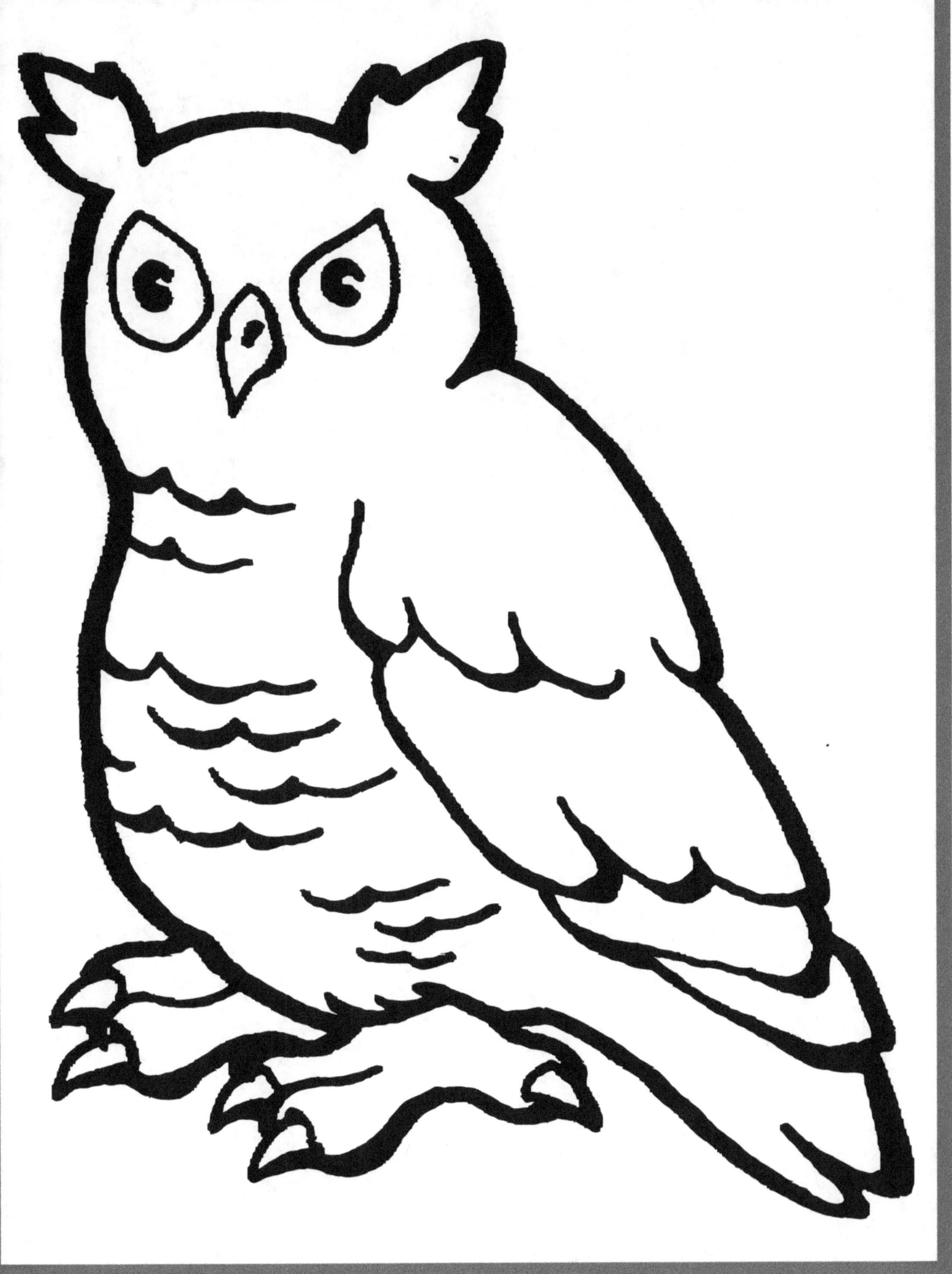

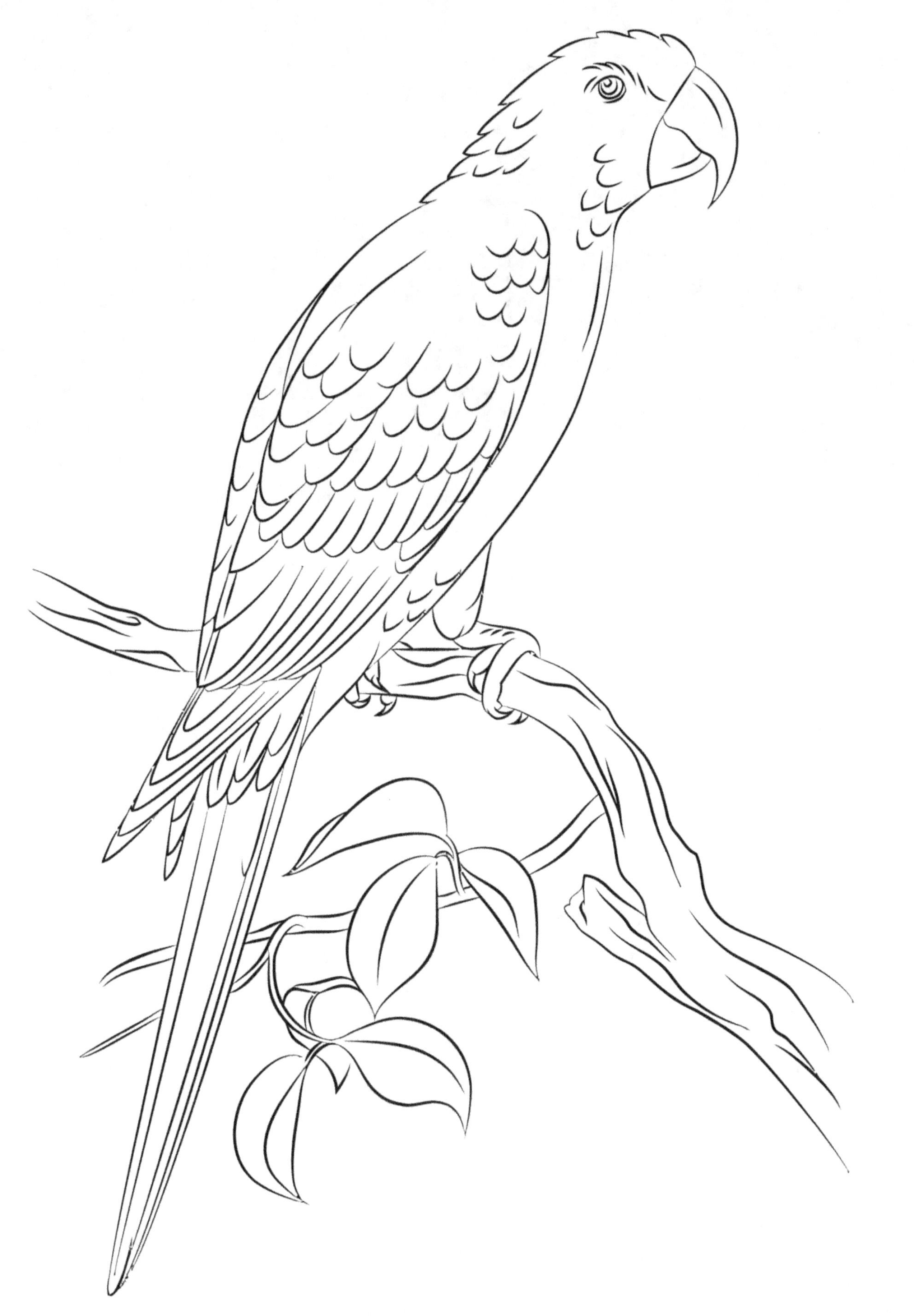

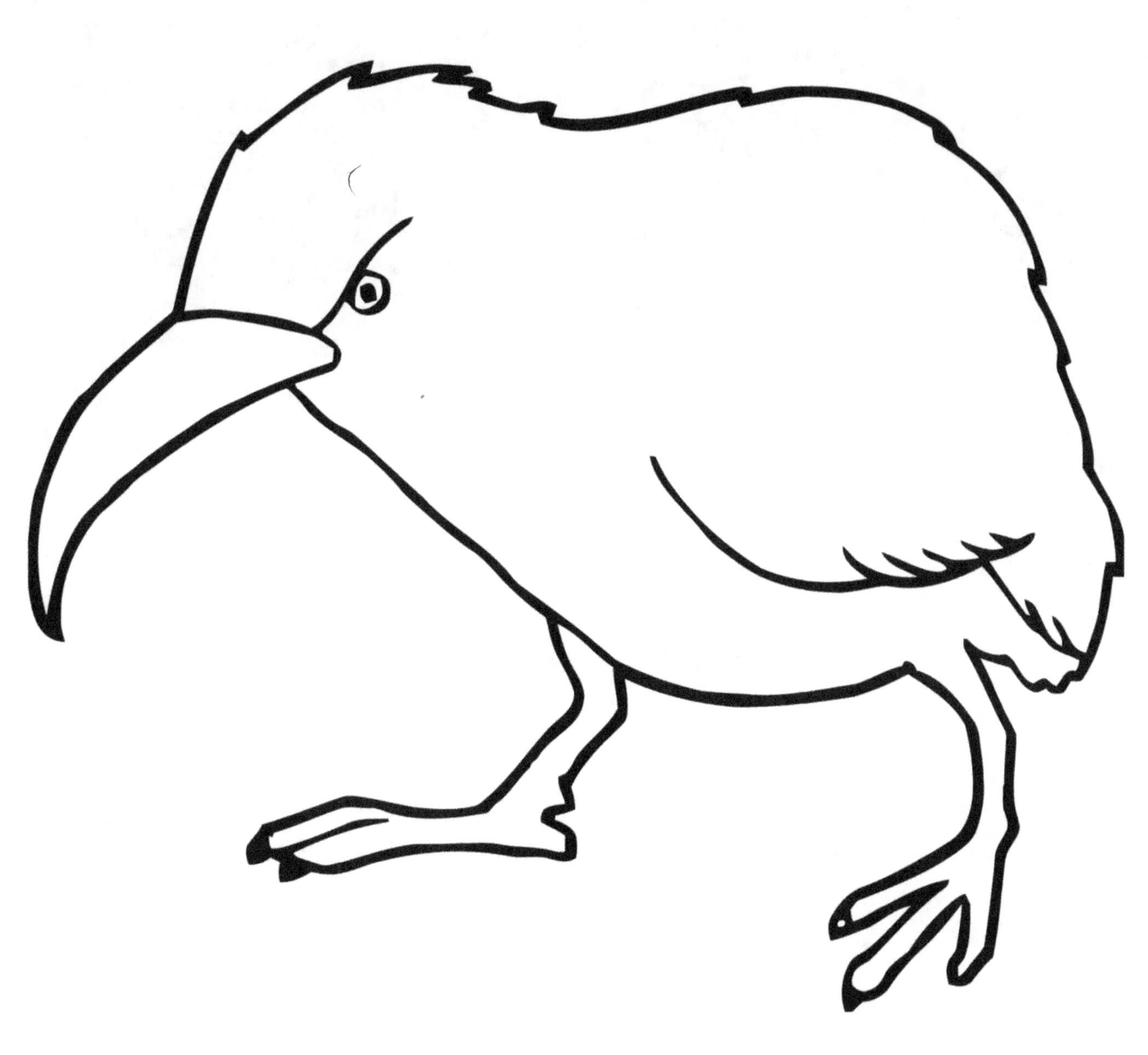

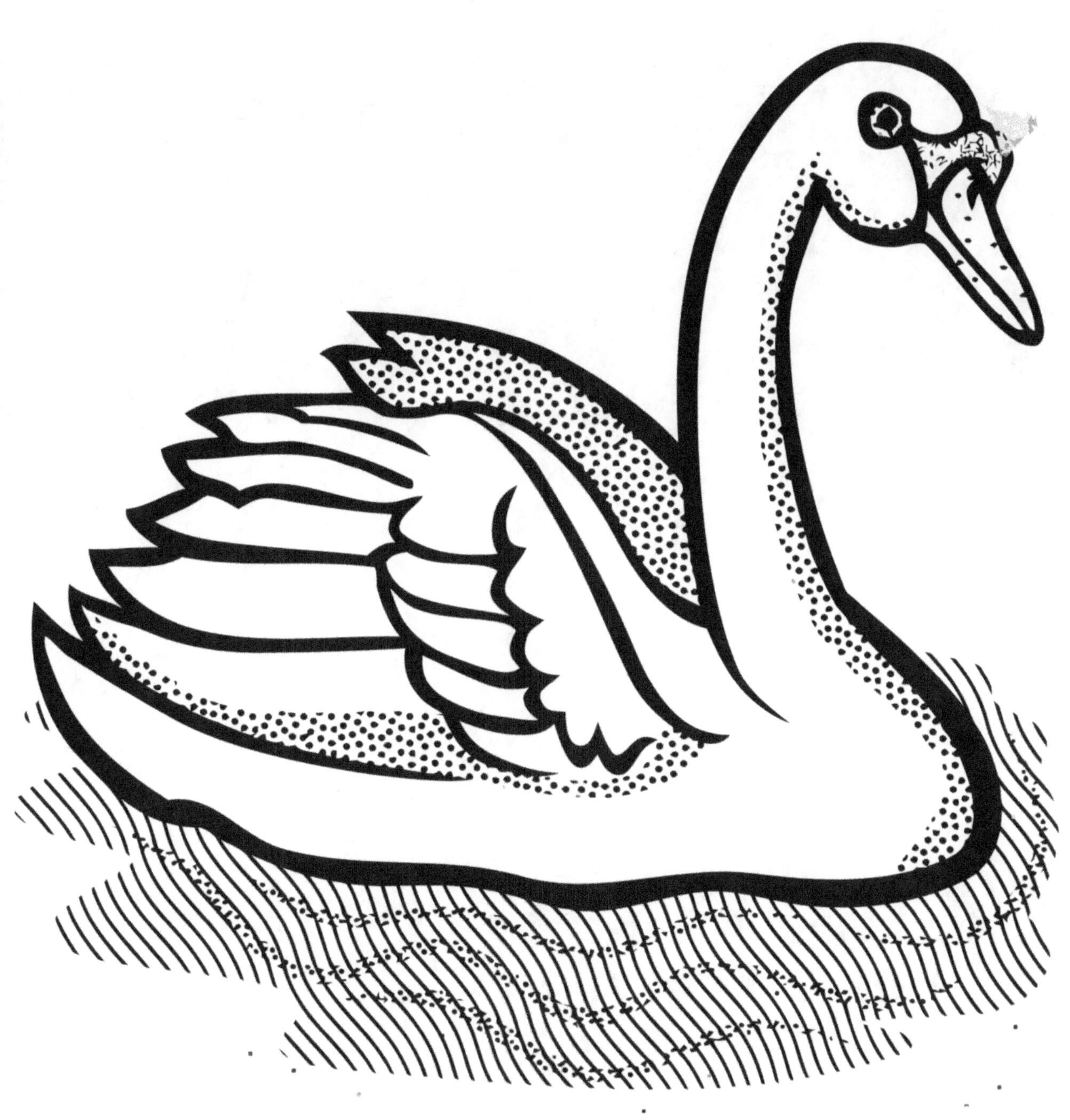

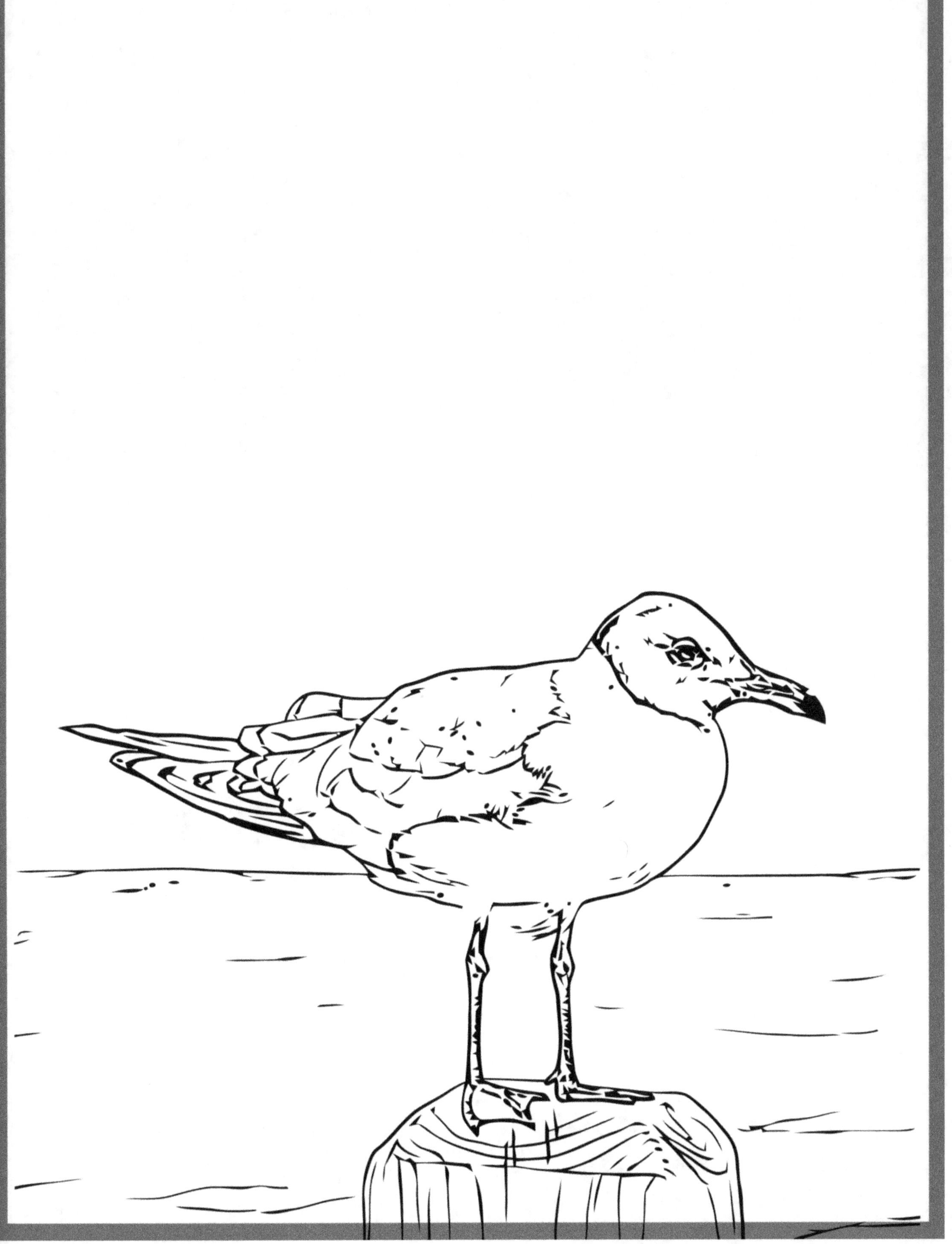

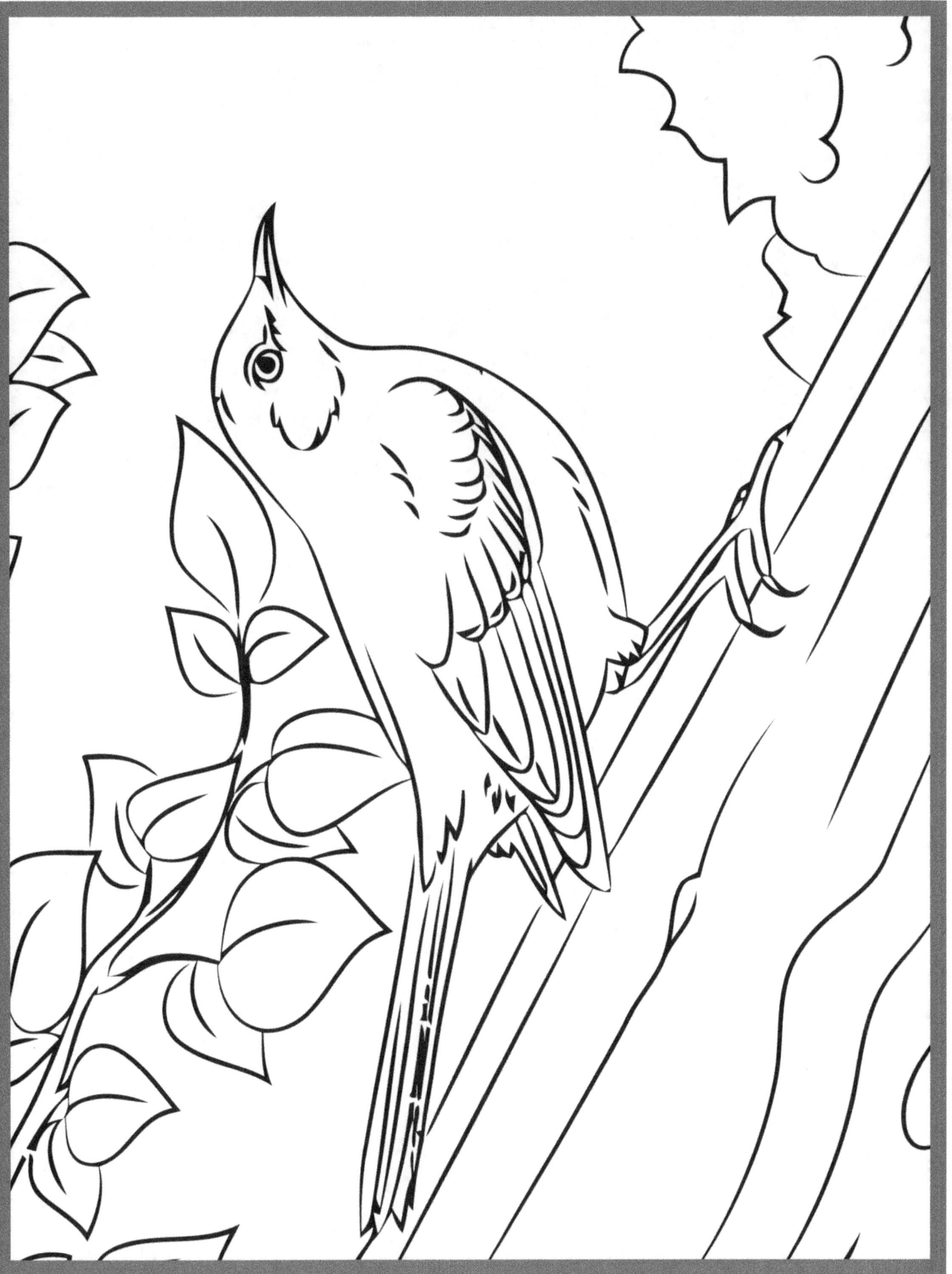

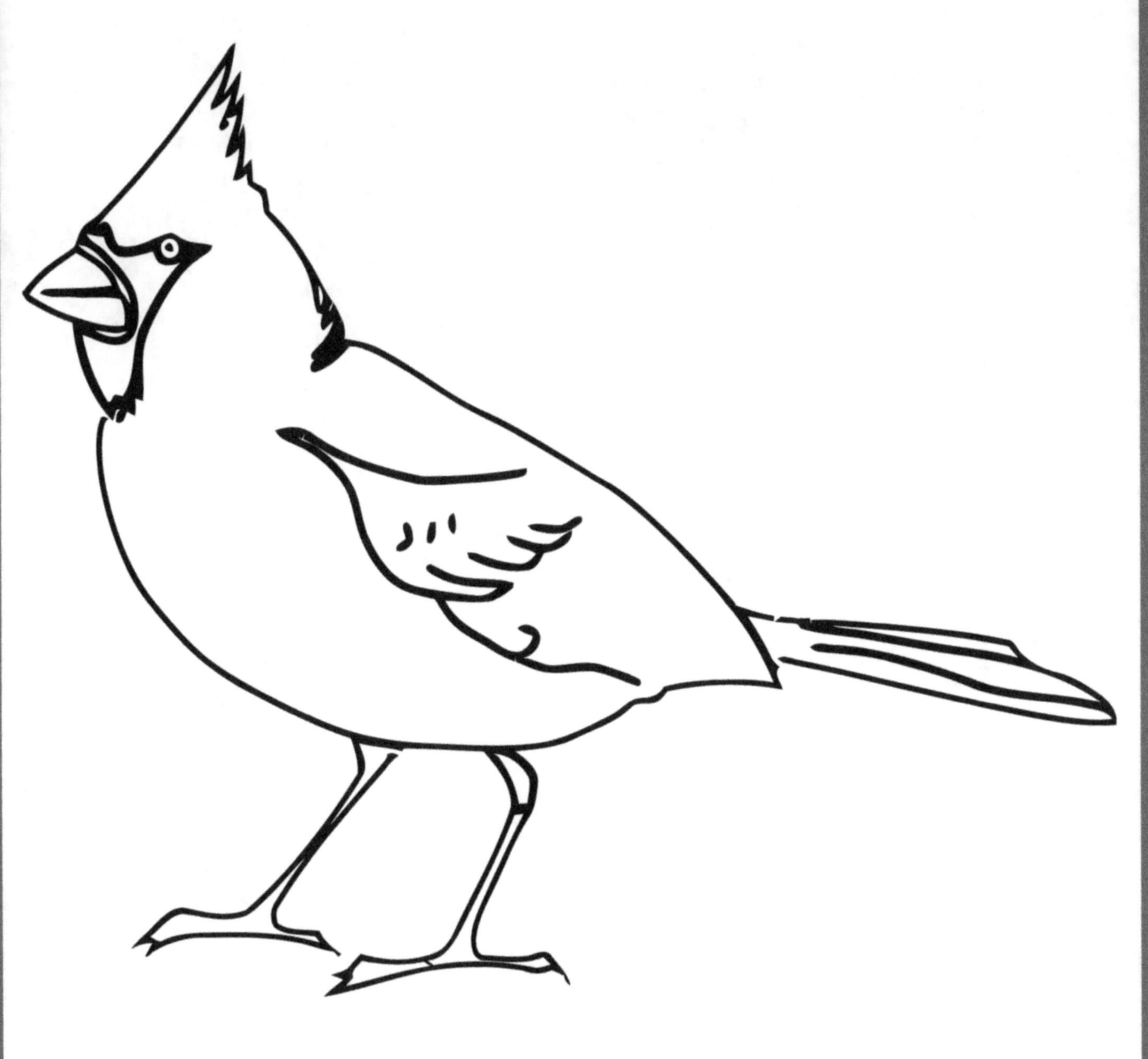

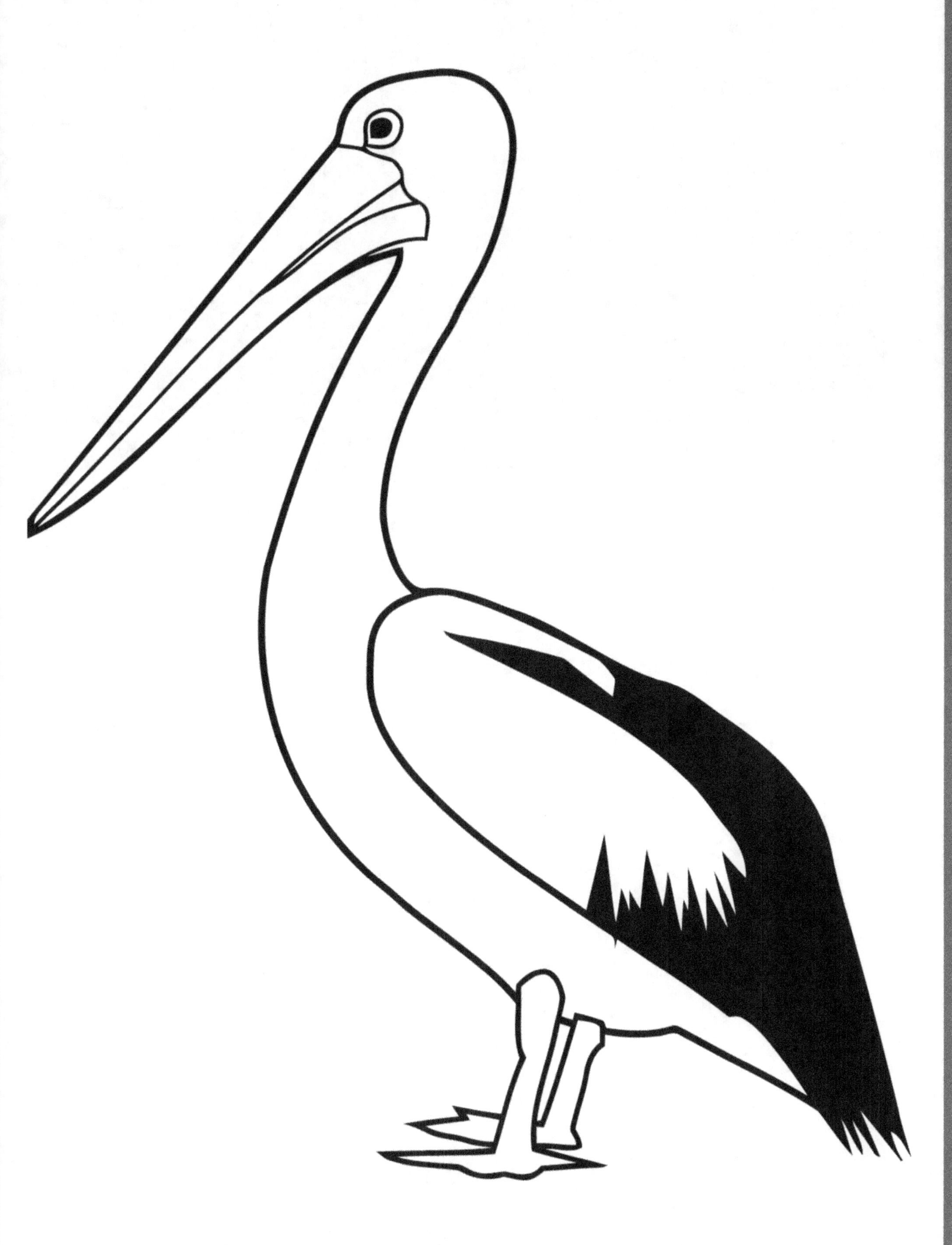

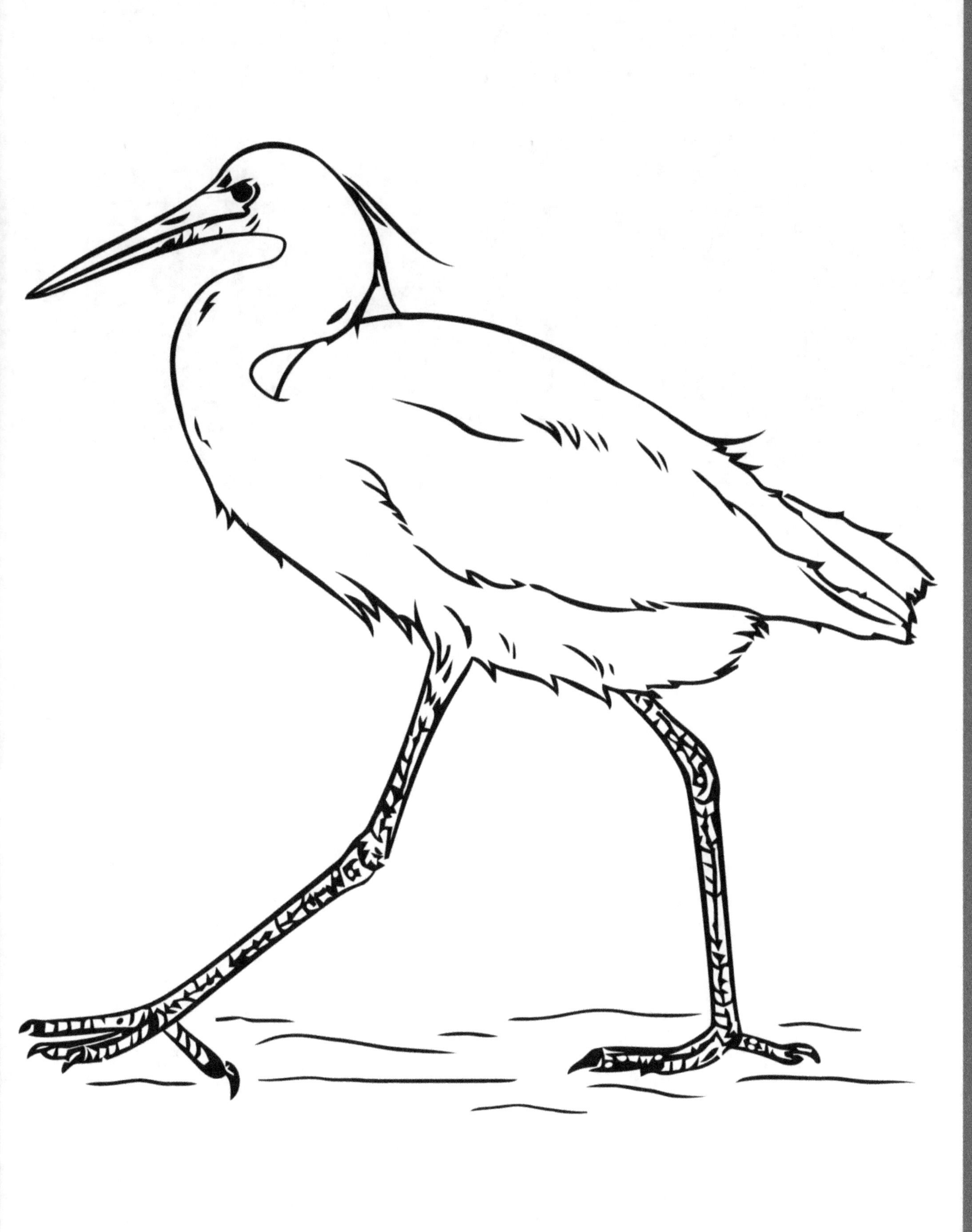

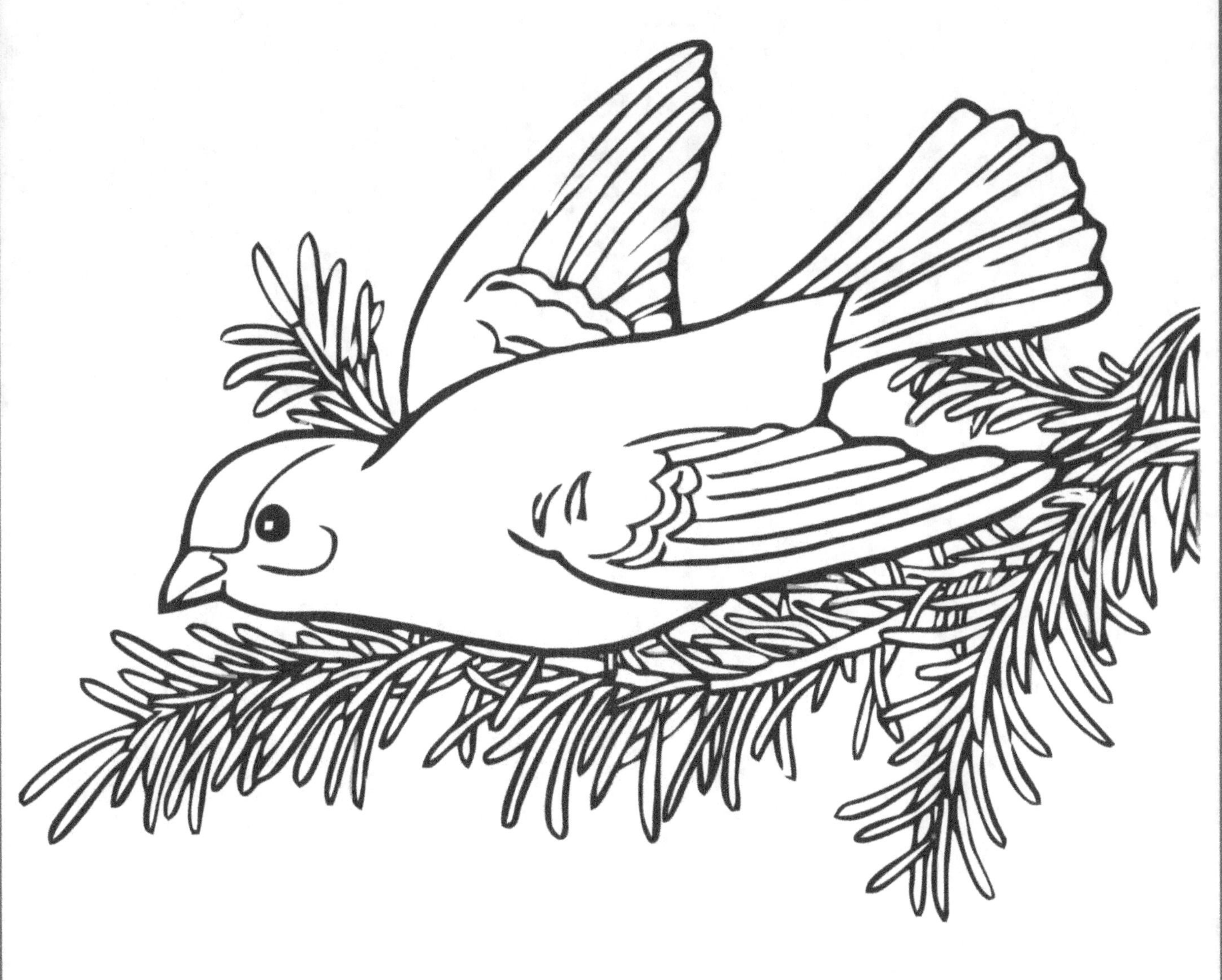

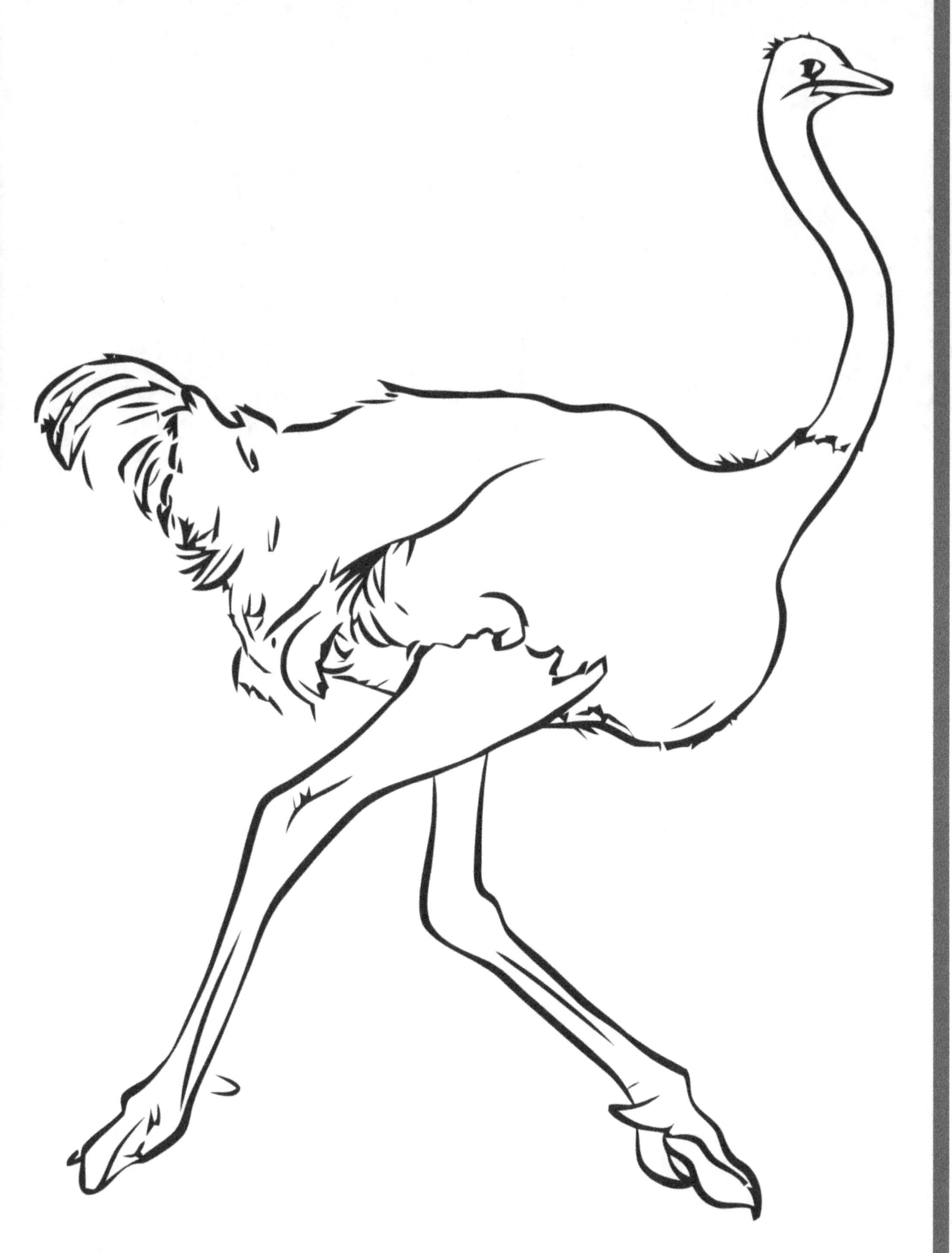

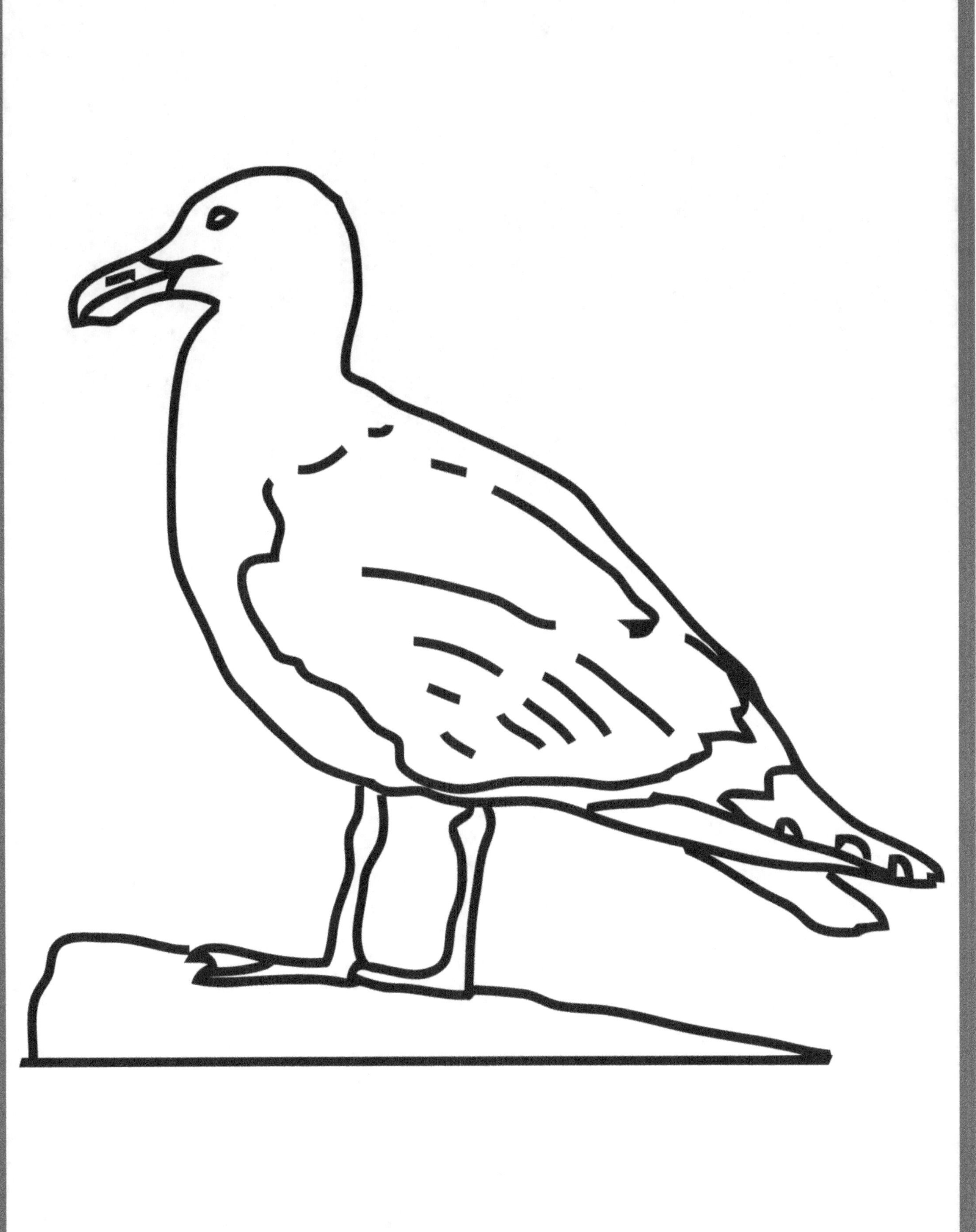

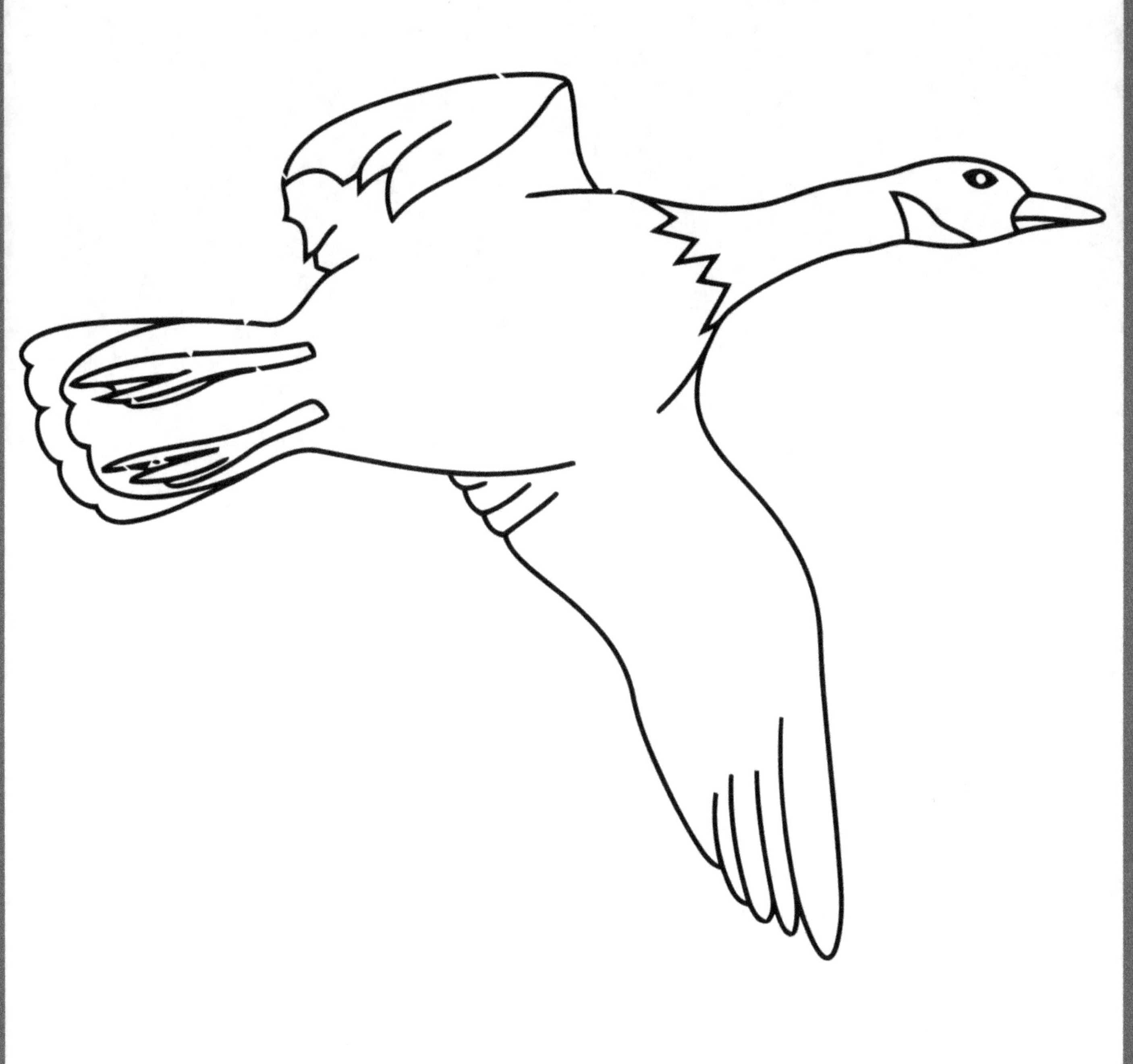

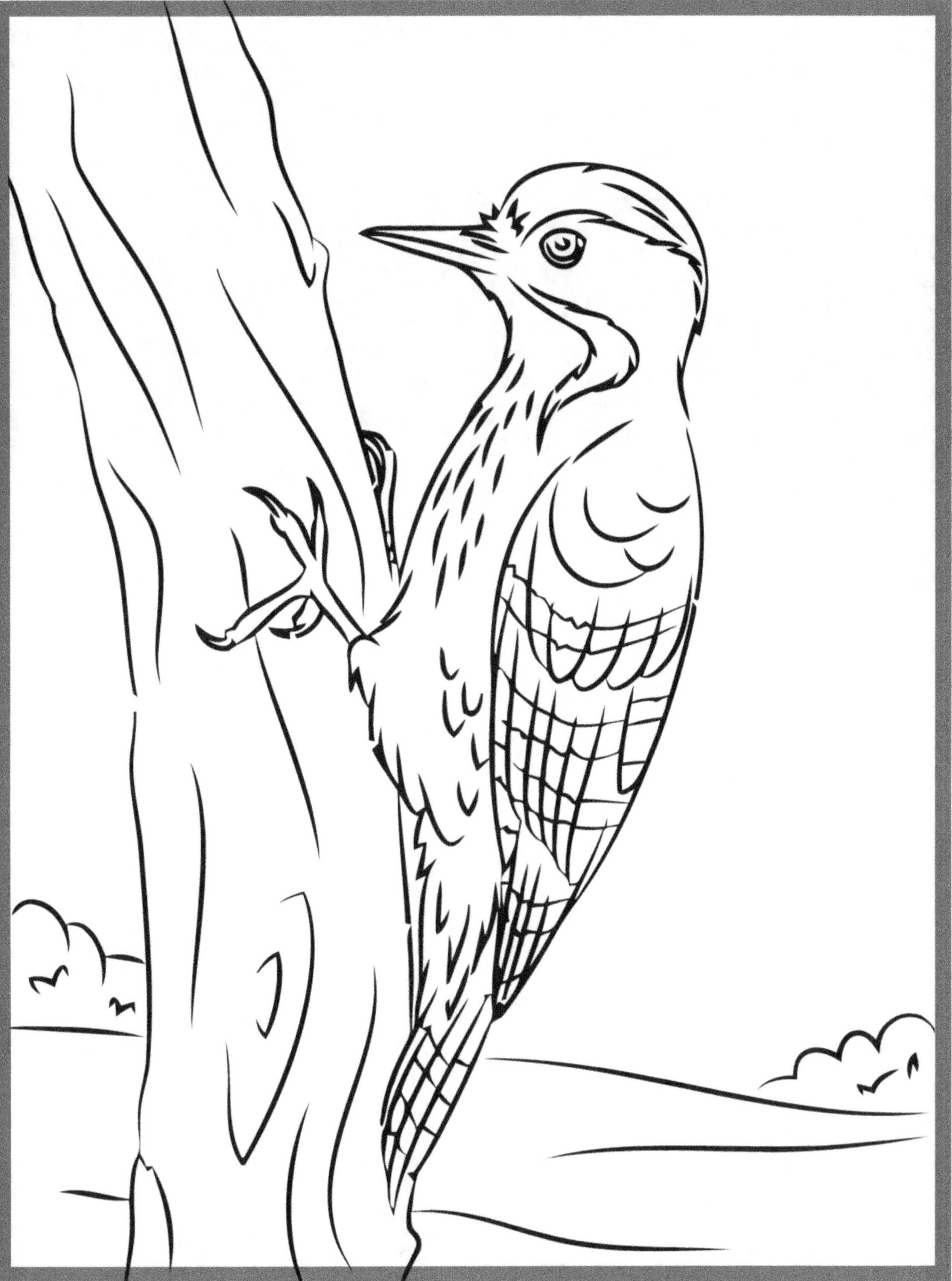

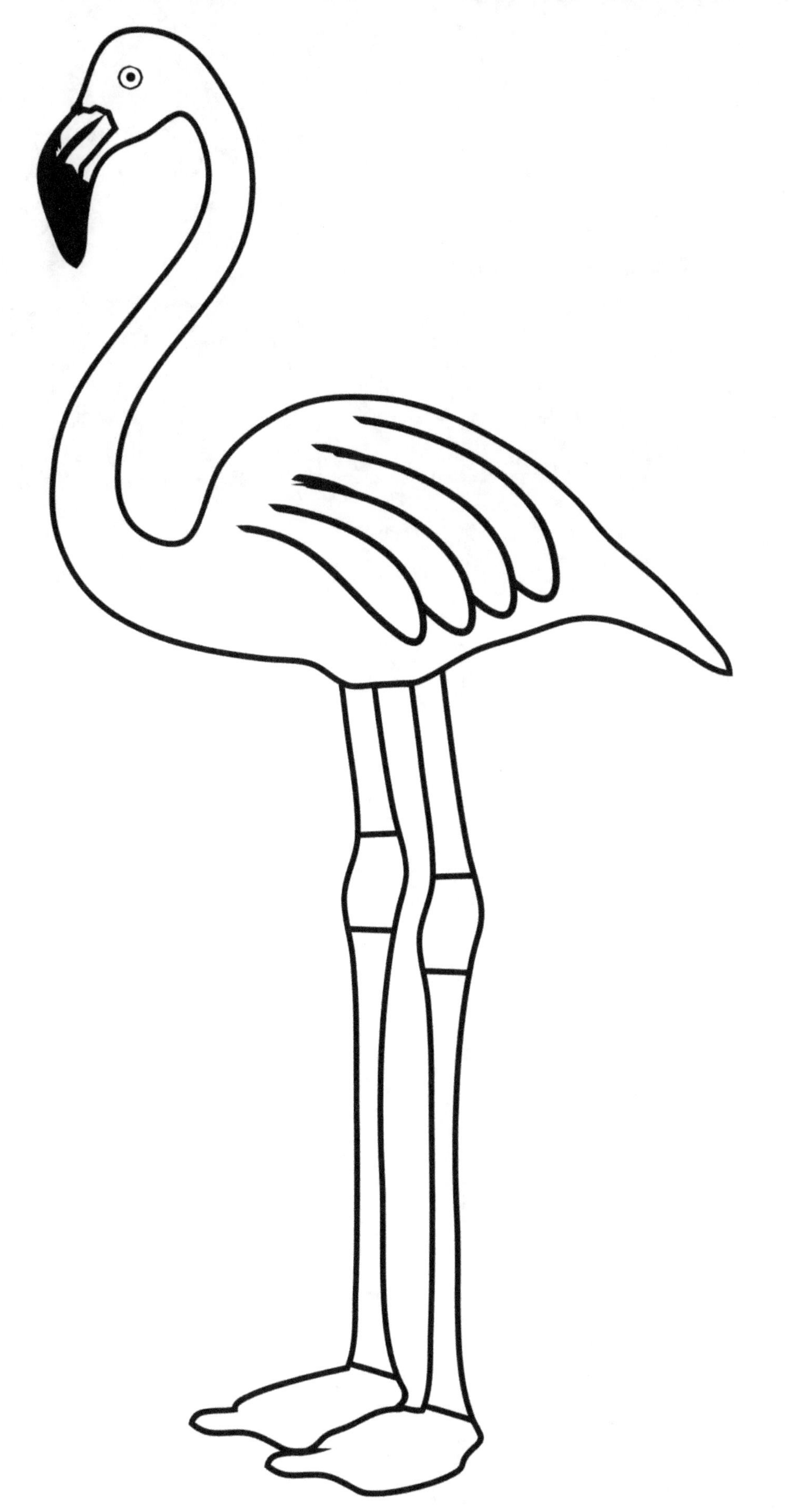

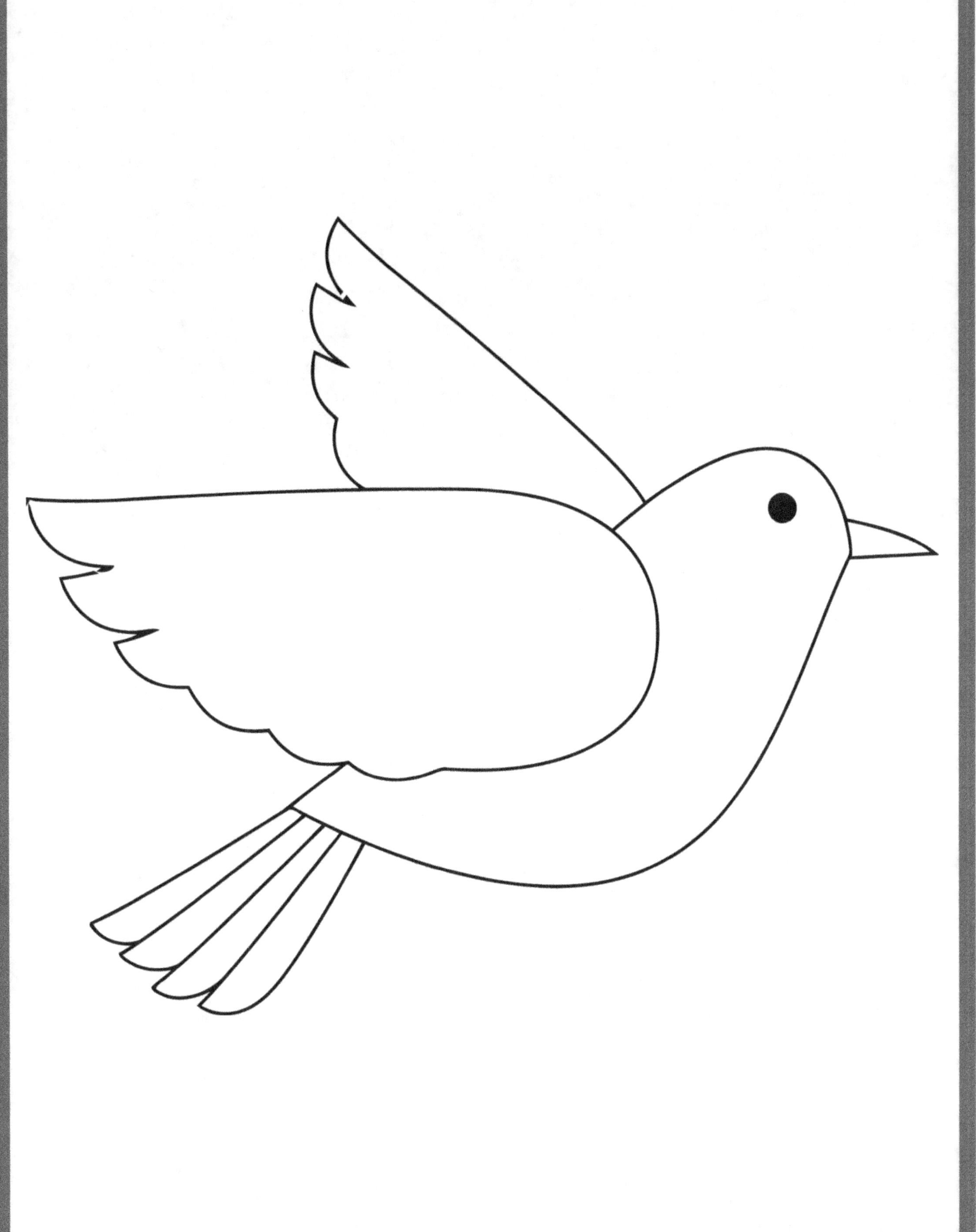

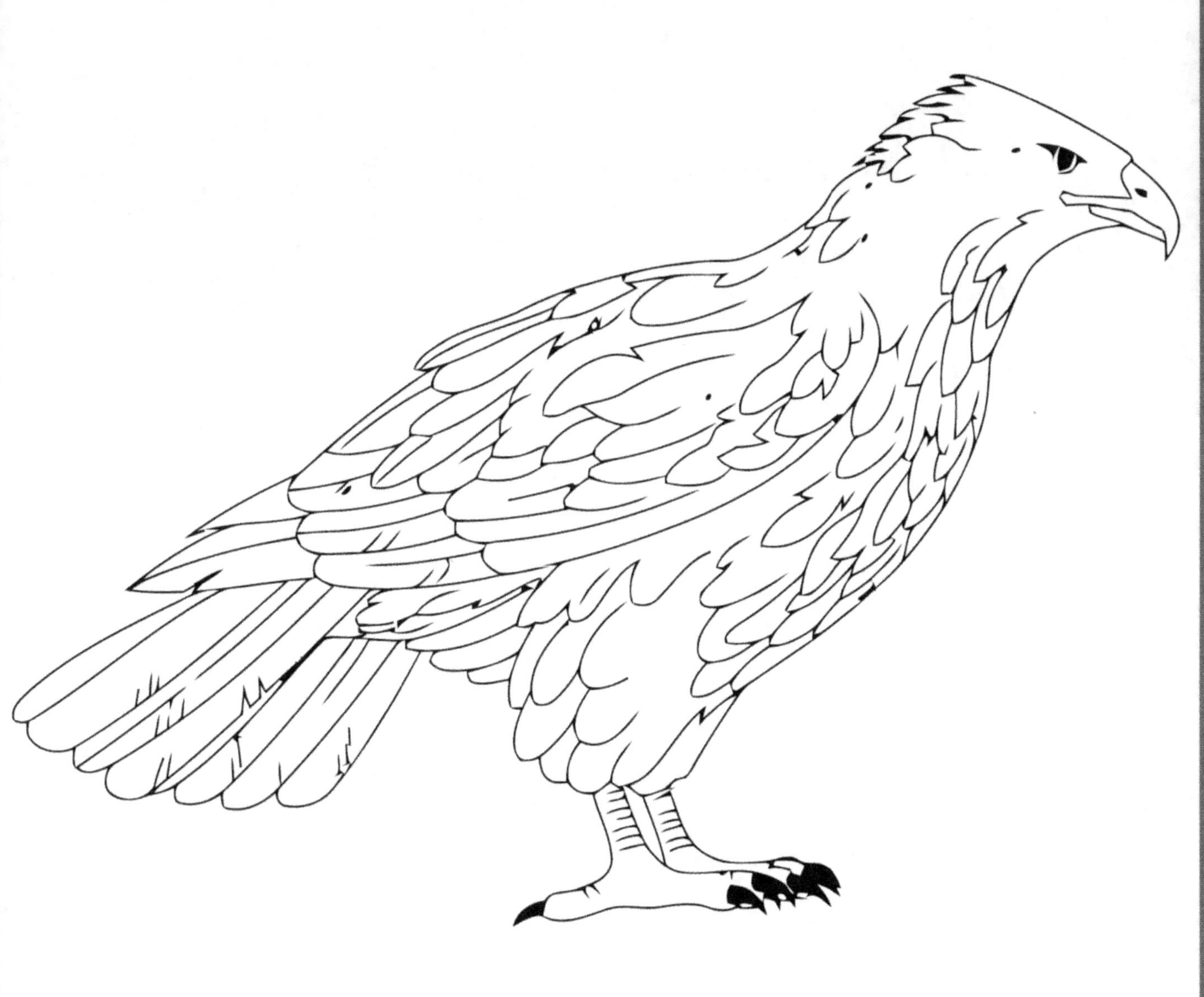

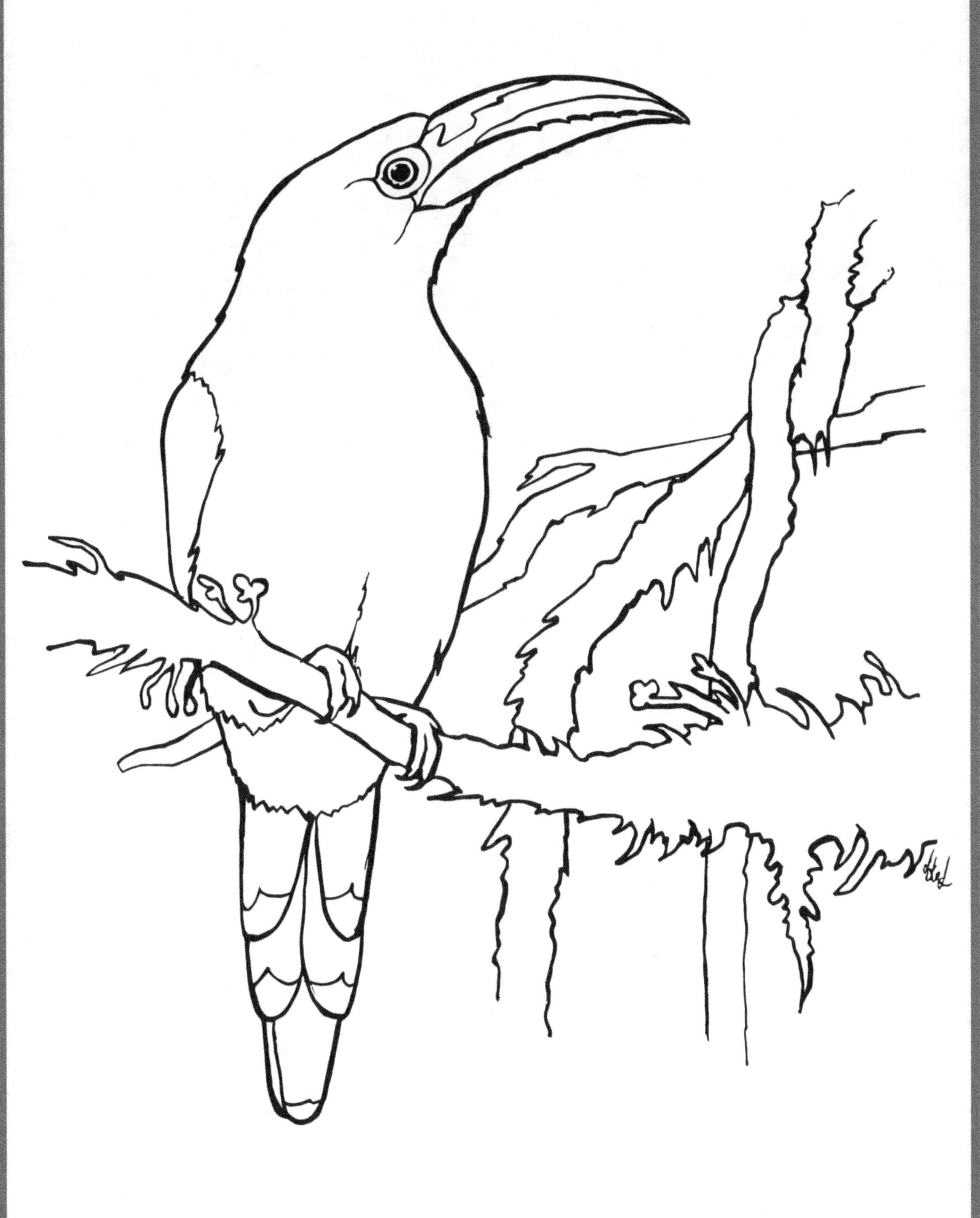

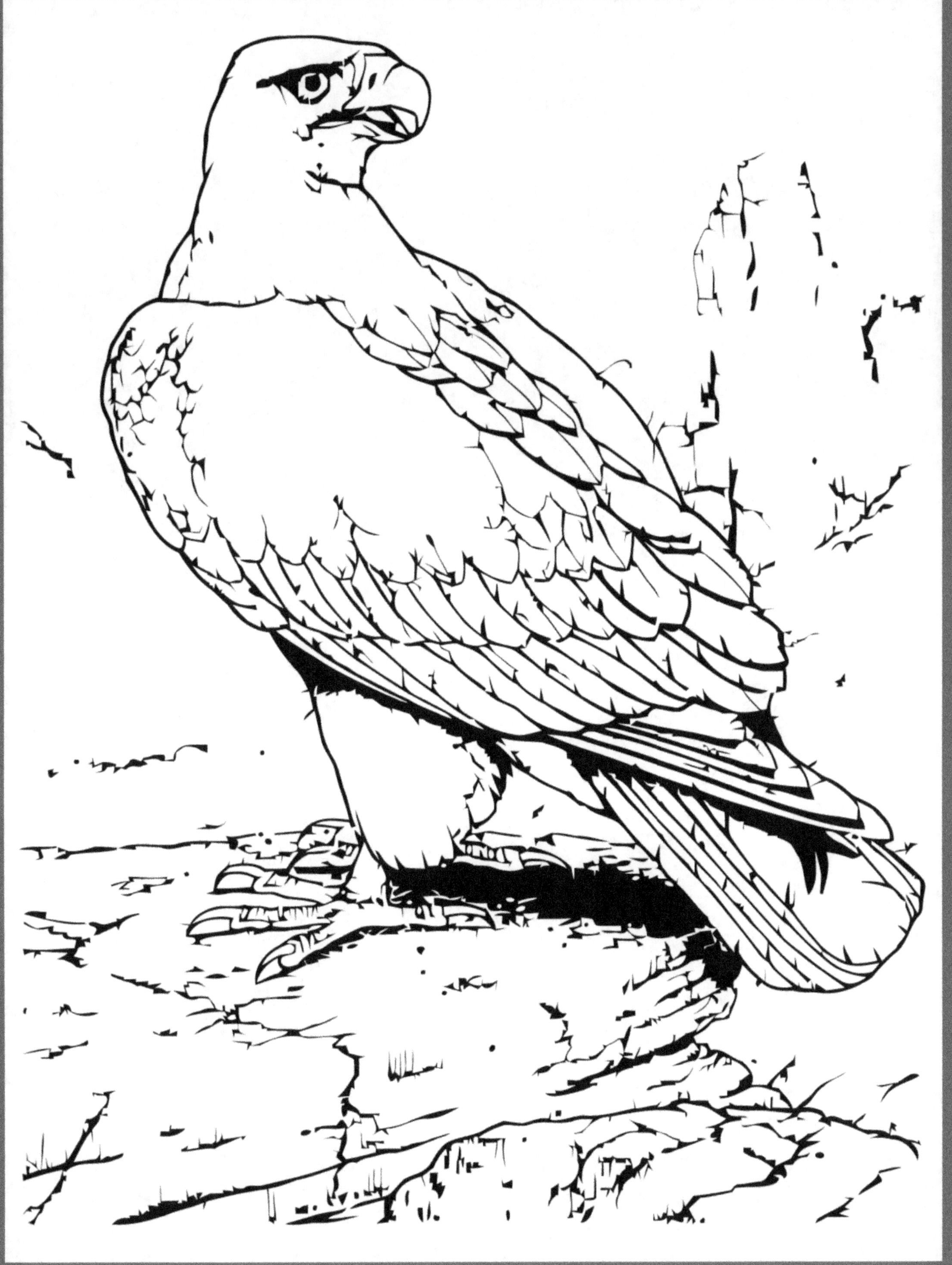

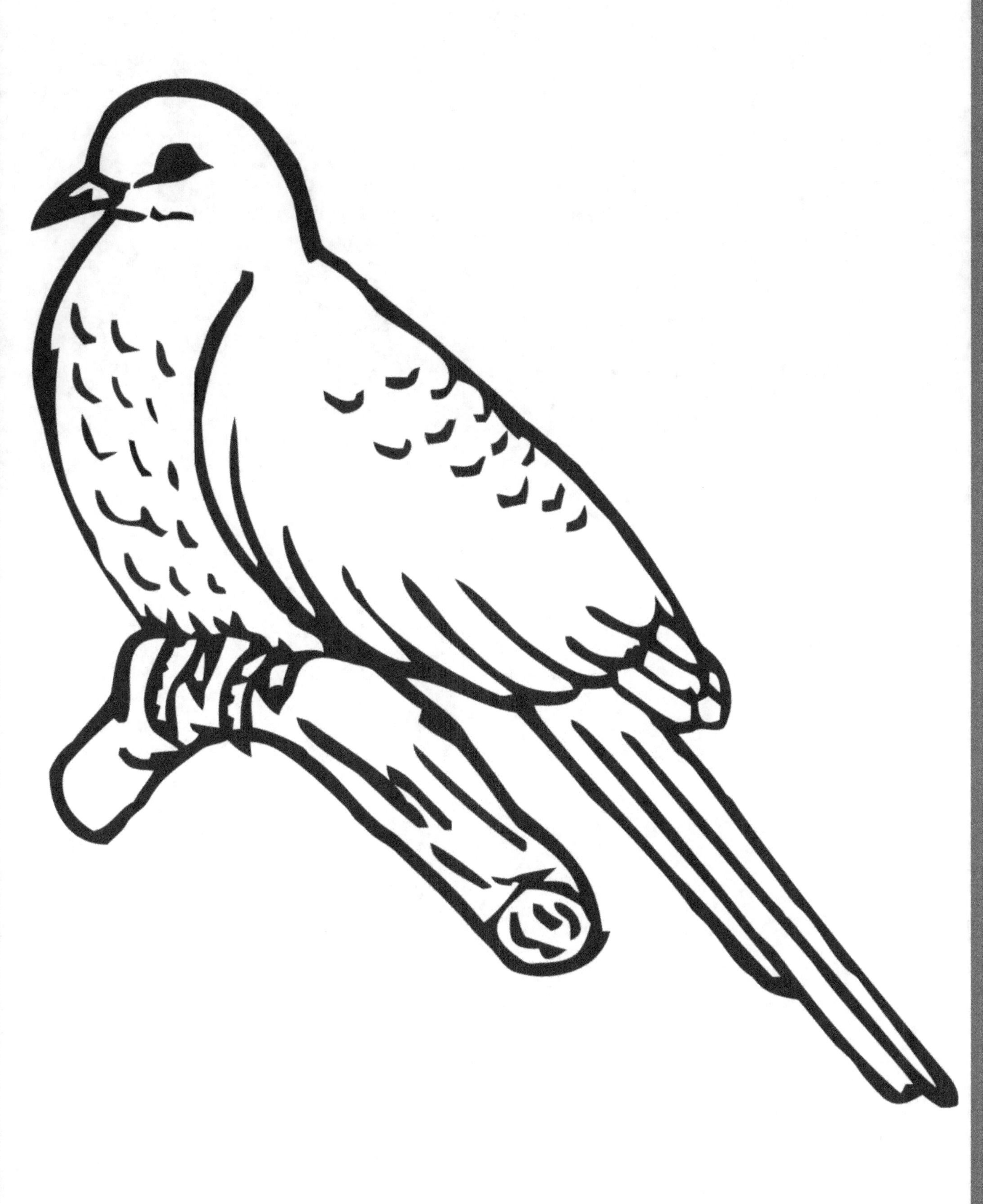

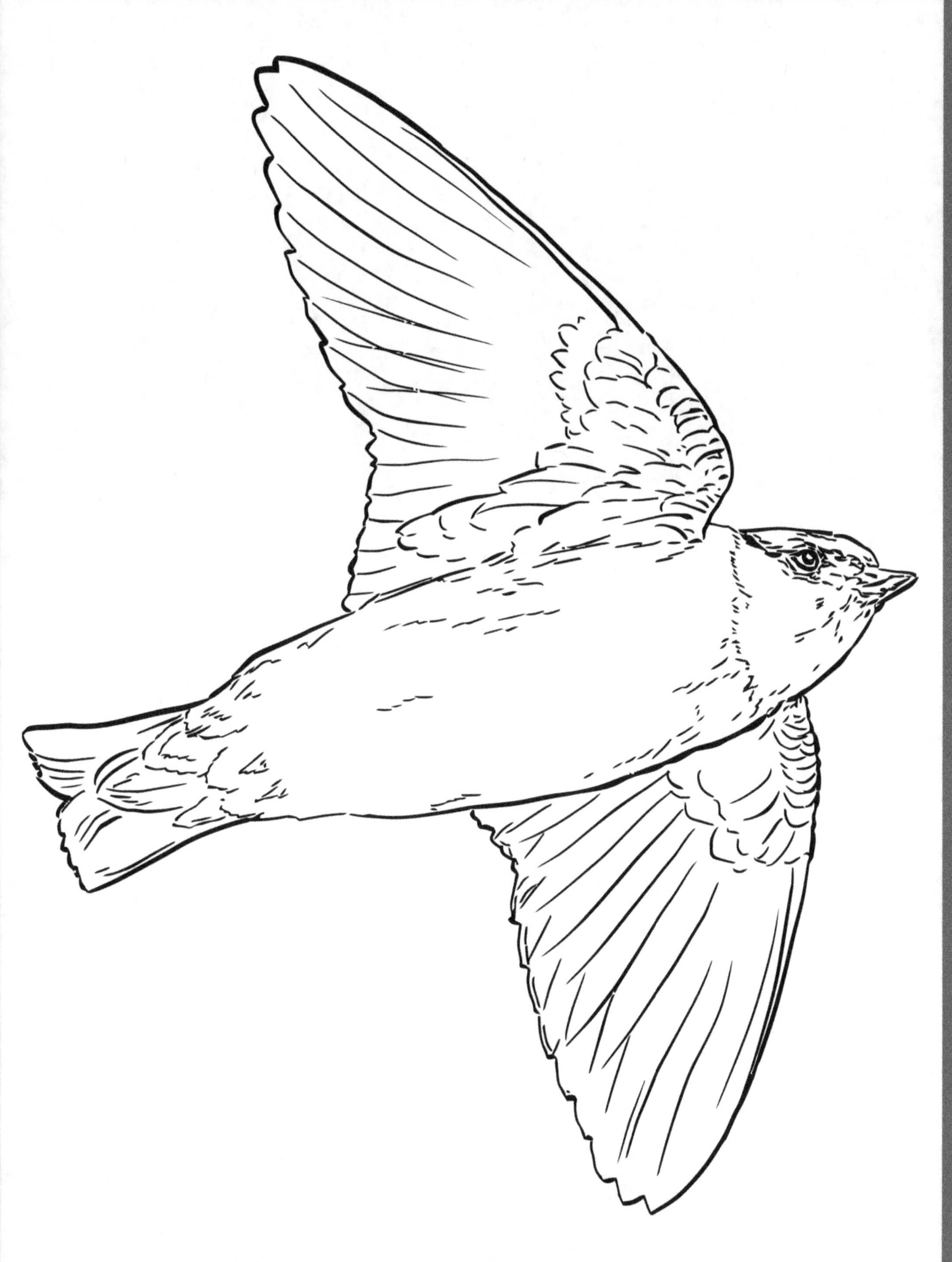

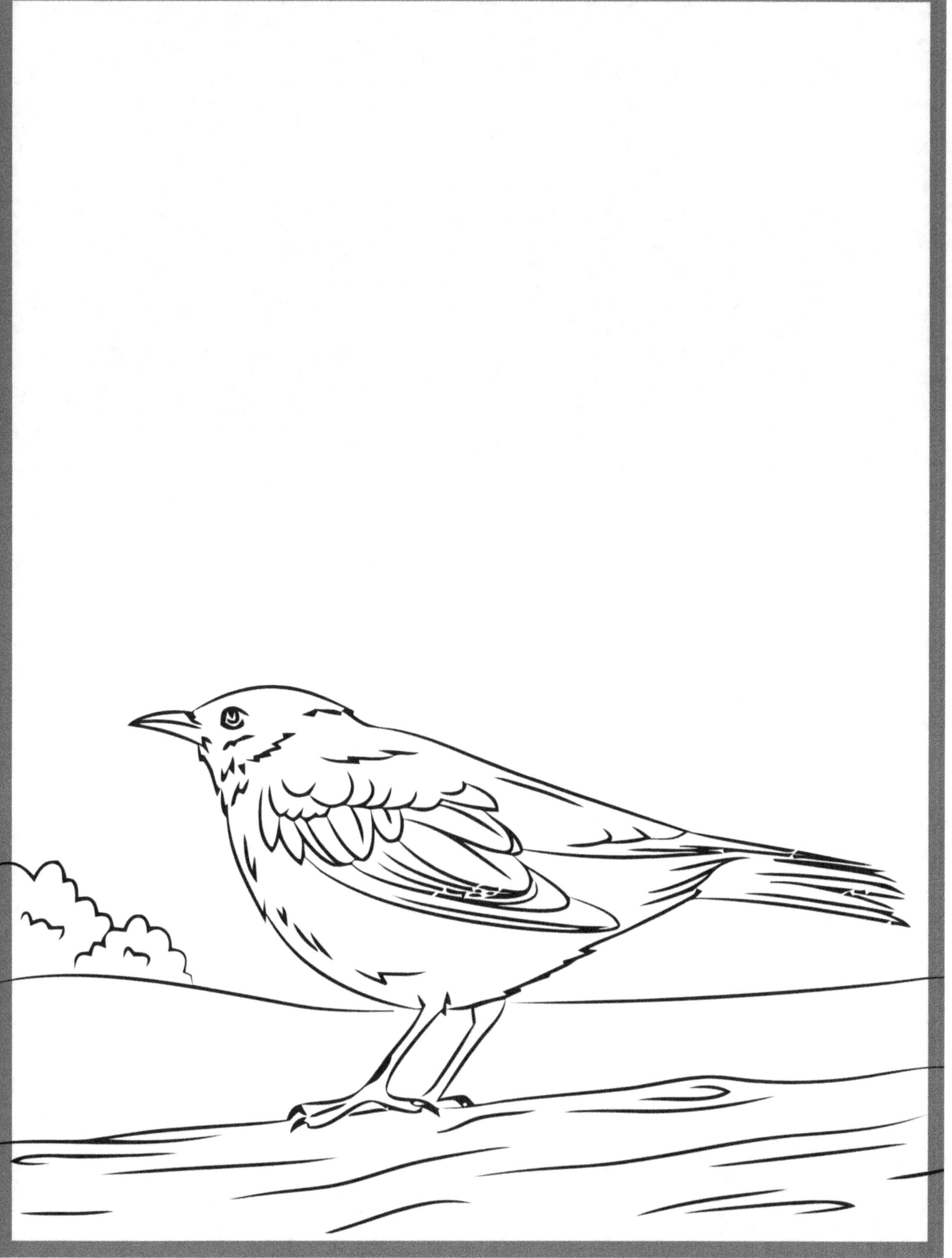

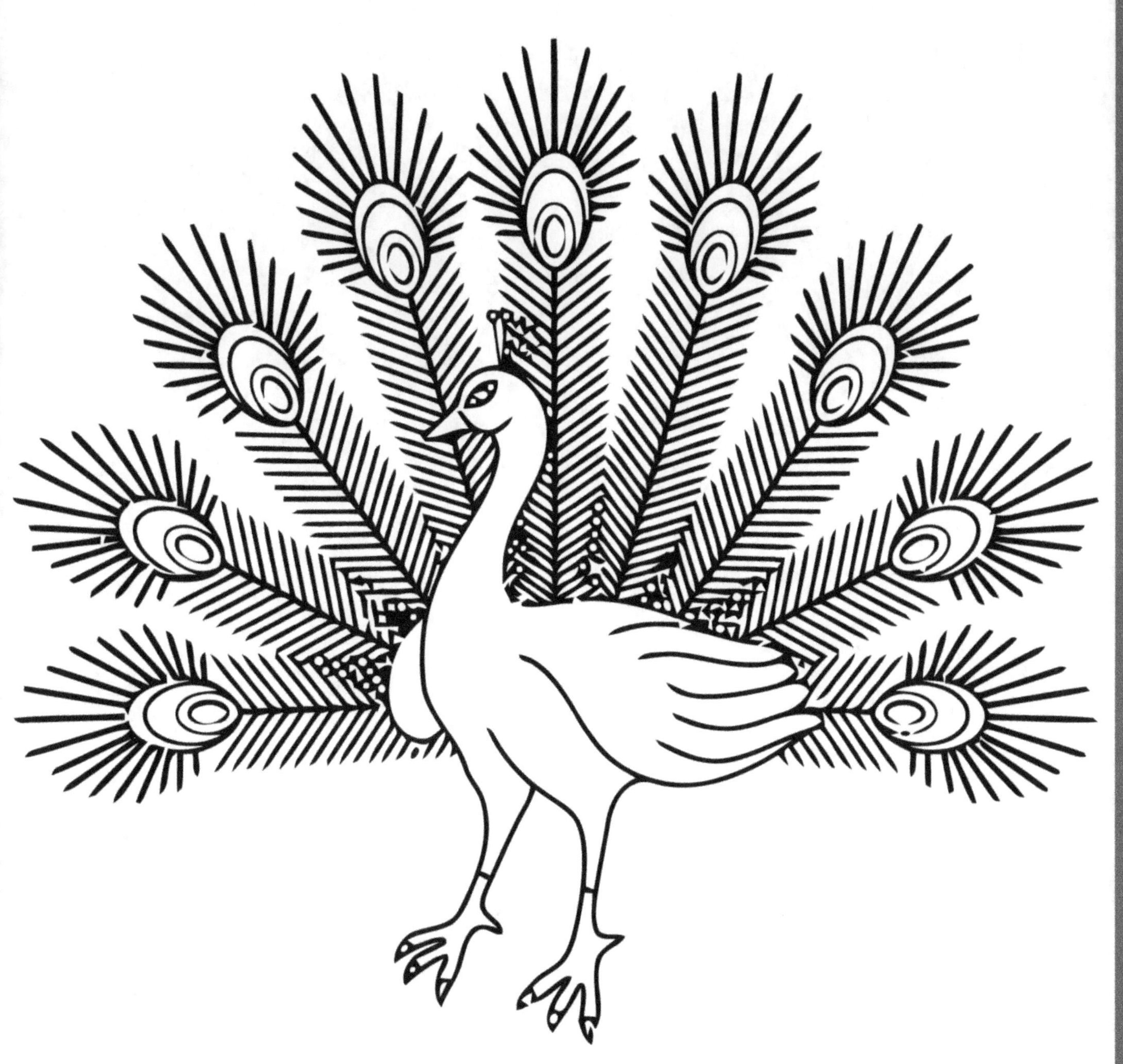

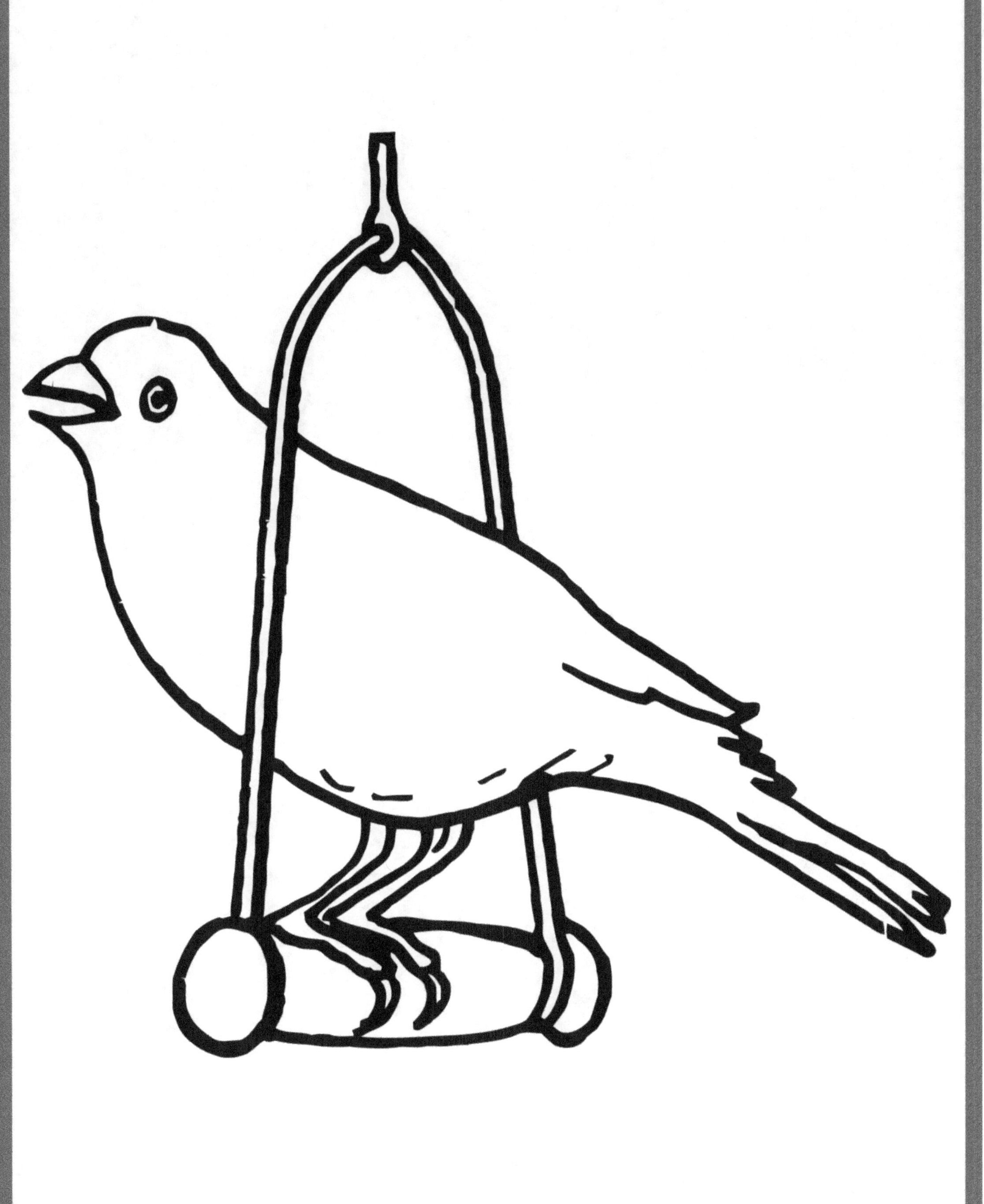

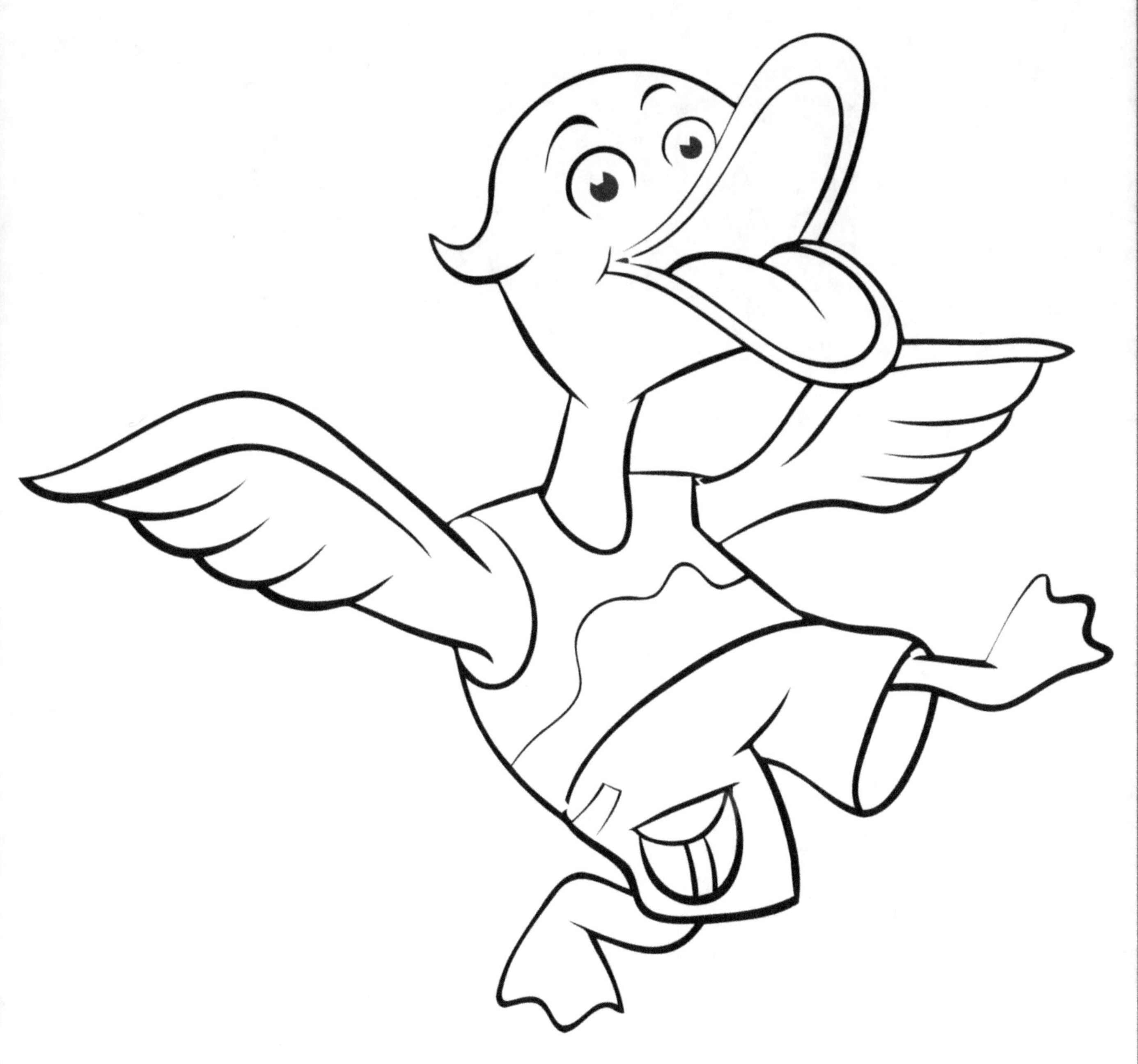

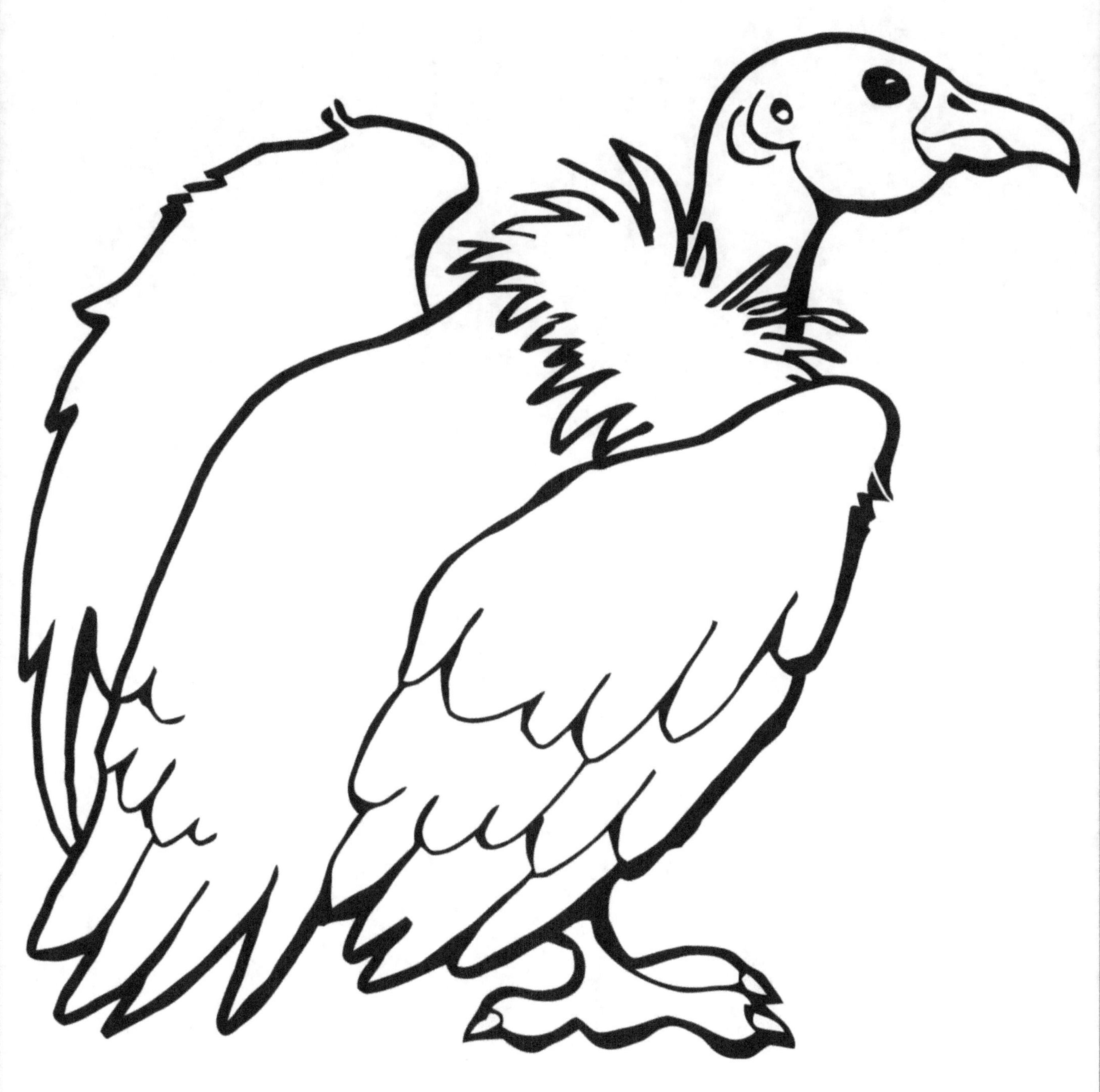

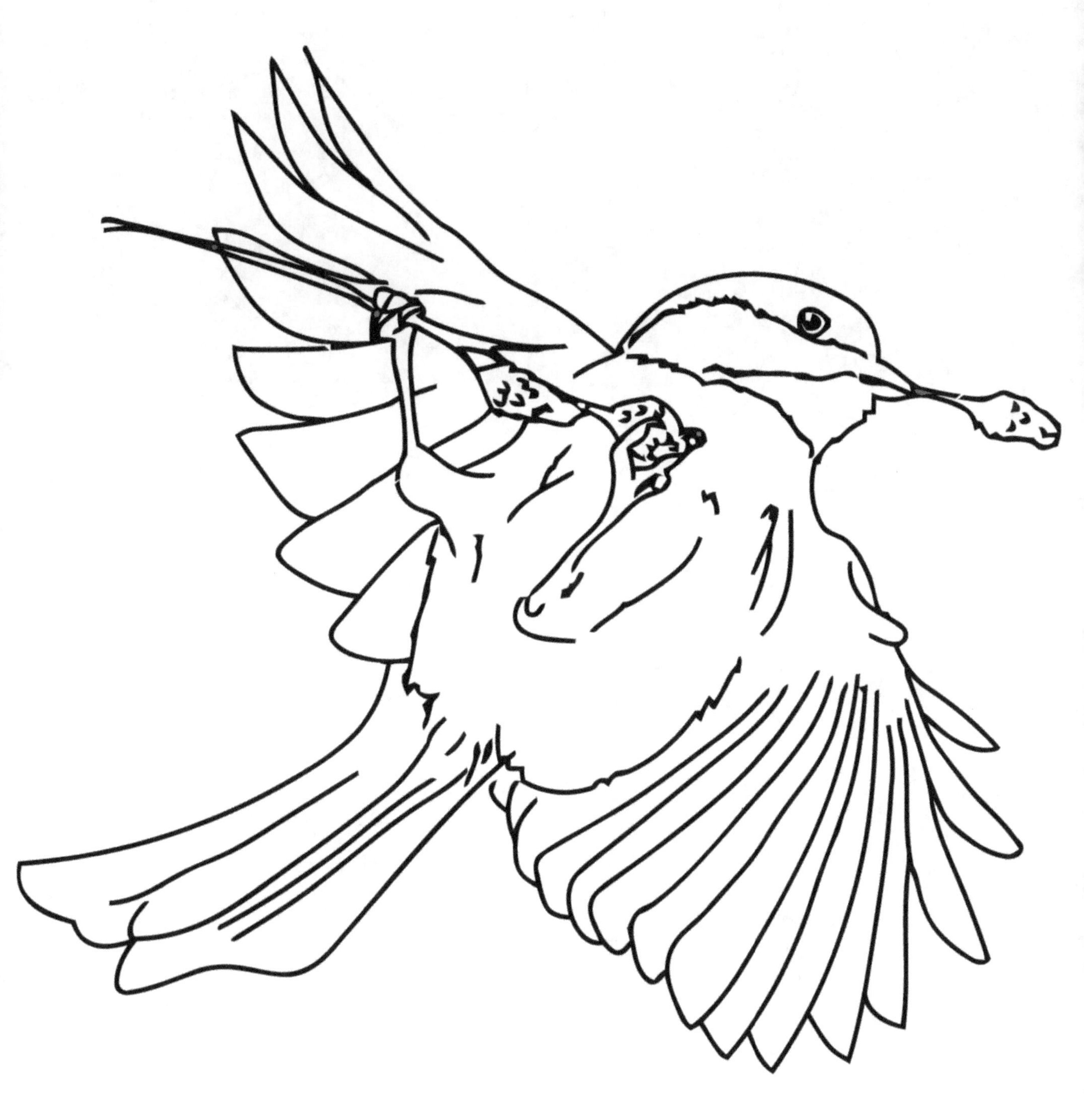